THE LIBERAL IN THE LOOKING-GLASS

THE LIBERAL
IN THE
LOOKING-GLASS

by Gregorio Marañón

The LONG HOUSE, Inc.

1964

COPYRIGHT 1964

The LONG HOUSE, Inc.
PUBLISHERS
NEW CANAAN, CONNECTICUT

Cover design by John O.C. McCrillis
Printed in the United States of America
$2.00

Foreign Editions

France   Nouvelles Éditions Latines
1961   1, rue Palatine, Paris 6ème

Spain   Publicaciones de la OID
1961   San Salvador, 3, Madrid

CONTENTS

This essay, first published in Paris in 1937, was written by the highly respected and internationally known Spanish intellectual, Dr. Gregorio Marañón. In 1961, in both Paris and Madrid, the essay was republished in book form. The first American edition appeared in 1964.

Translated from the original French.
by Denise Loire, in collaboration
with John Howland Snow.

PROLOGUE

The opera *Andrea Chénier,* by Umberto Giordano, is based upon the life of a great French liberal and patriot, Andrea Chénier, who was guillotined during The Terror which grew out of the Revolution of 1789.

The PROLOGUE to *The Liberal in the Looking-Glass* is taken from *Andrea Chénier,* Act III. In this scene, Gérard, one of Chénier's closest friends, is writing the indictment which leads to the latter's execution. L'Incredibile, a socially prominent woman spy, is looking over Gérard's shoulder and dictating the terms.

Rendered from the Italian
BY JOHN HOWLAND SNOW

GÉRARD

(riprende la penna; riflette)

Nemico della patria?!

(ride)

È veccia fiaba! . . .

(scrive)

Beatamente ognor la beve il popolo.

(scrive)

Nato a Constantinopoli? . . .

(riflette, poi esclama e scrive:)

Straniero!
Studiò a Saint-Cyr? . . .
Soldato! . . .
Di Dumouriez un complice?
Traditore!
È poeta?
Sovvertitor di cuori e di costumi! . . .
Poi . . . m'ha ferito? . . . Scrivo "odio
    politico!"

*(ma a quest' ultima accusa la pen-
na gli fugge dalle mani)*

Un di m' era di gioja passar fra
    morte e morte
fra gli odi e le vendette, puro, inno-
    cente e forte!
Dà sangue or fango e lacrime la mia
    superba idea . . .
Un vil piccino io sono! . . .
Gigante mi credea! . . .
Io sono sempre un servo! . . .
Ho mutato padrone! . . .
Sono il servo obbediente di violenta
    passione!
Ah, peggio! . . . Uccido e tremo!
Cosi fra sangue e fango
senza coraggio passo, e, mentre uccido,
    io piango!

Io della Redentrice figlio pel primo ho
    udito
il grido suo pel mondo e vi ho il mio
    grido unito . . .
Or smarrita ho la fede nel sognato
    destino? . . .
Com' era irradiato di gloria il mio
    cammino! . . .
La coscienza nei cuori ridestar de le
    genti! . . .
Raccogliere le lacrime dei vinti e sof-
    ferenti! . . .
Vincere le tenèbre! . . . Diritto la Sa-
    pienza! . . .
Dovere l'Eguaglianza! . . . L'amore In-
    telligenza! . . .
Fare del mondo un Pantheon! . . . Gli
    uomini in dii mutare
e in un sol bacio e abbraccio tutte le
    genti amare! . . .
Ah, di Chénier la voce fu, voce di
    poeta
che luminosa allora tracciata m'ha la
    meta.
Or rinnego il poeta? — Rinnego il
    santo grido
che m'ha redento? — Ah in lui la
    mia coscienza uccido!
Sol l'odio! . . . L'odio! . . . L'odio! . . .
    Io d'odio ho colmo il cuore
e chi cosi mi ha reso, fiera ironia!
    è l'amore!
Sono un voluttuoso! . . . Ecco il nuovo
    padrone;
il Senso! . . . — Bugia tutto! Sol vero
    la Passione!

GÉRARD

Enemy of the Fatherland?! Hah! That ancient fable that forever the public swallows whole . . . Born in Constantinople? Amazing! Graduate of Saint-Cyr? A soldier! Accomplice of Dumouriez? Traitor! *** He shot me? I write, "political hatred!"

But, at this final accusation, the pen falls from his hand and Gérard begins his soliloquy:

Once upon a time I joyfully sped, above all death, above the hatreds and the vengeances, pure and innocent, and oh, so strong. Far was I from the blood and tears of others, yet now, from this magnificence, I am become once more a wretched slave.

Magnificent were my convictions, yet now I find myself no more than serf. What? I have but changed my masters.

I am become the cringing menial of outraged passion: Worse; even as I cause death I tremble. I move, thus spineless, from blood to ravishment, my tears of shame falling even as I utter the words of condemnation.

I, son of the Revolution, whose voice responded so eagerly to its first faint worldly cry — am I to see my faith betrayed by its own predestined course?

How irradiated with glory was to be my path — to help rekindle conscience in the hearts of all mankind; to help dry the tears of the vanquished and the oppressed; to banish the engulfing shadows; to enshrine resplendent Wisdom; to encompass benign Equality; to raise high the light of all Intelligence! I, who was to help make of this earth a Paradise! To make into gods its men, and, in one vast gesture of consummation to see all men embrace as brothers!

Ah, but this was the voice of Chénier, the voice of the poet which had emblazoned my way.

How, now, have I fallen. Do I denounce the holy call which had forsooth redeemed me? Verily in him it is my own conscience that I slay.

Hate! It is no more than hate! Hate!! Hate!!! I, who have filled my heart with bitterness, and this bitterness — oh, irony — is destined to fulfill my love.

I am become a base voluptuary. Lo, I find my new master — and it is Passion. All else is false! There remains to me this one last verity, and it is Passion!

GREGORIO MARAÑÓN, 1887-1960

Written especially for the American edition by his son, Gregorio Marañón Moya

GREGORIO MARAÑÓN was born in Madrid on the 19th day of May, 1887. He died in that city on the 27th of March, 1960.

His youth was influenced decisively by two famous men, Menéndez y Pelayo and Pérez Galdós. Both were his father's intimate friends. They nurtured the awakening of his spirit; they watched over its development; and they encouraged him as he became absorbed in the world of letters and science.

In medicine, he was the favorite pupil of the greatest teachers of his day: Olóriz, Madinaveitia, San Martín and Cajal. His passion for research showed itself early, and it never flagged. He was one of the early specialists in endocrinology and became one of its masters. His teaching, his lectures, books and essays brought him worldwide fame, and degrees *Honoris Causa* were bestowed upon him by many of the world's great universities, among them Coimbra, Oporto, Milan, the Sorbonne, and almost every institution of higher learning in Latin America. A Chair of Internal Medicine was created especially for him at the University of Madrid.

The use he made of his time was little short of amazing. The extraordinary capacity for work with which he was endowed, his prodigious intellect, his exacting methodology, and his faculty of concentration and of assimilating knowledge enabled him to carry on work which was as diverse as it was majestic.

As an historian, he had no equal in Spain during the present century — Menéndez Pelayo and Menéndez Pidal excepted. His biographies — Henry IV of Castille, the Count-Duke of Olivares, Tiberius, Luis Vives, Antonio Pérez, the three Vélez — created a new genre in historical study. His scrupulously scientific documentation revealed men and events in true perspective vis-à-vis their times, and his clear, humanistic style brought to the works a success unprecedented in the publishing annals of Spain.

His essays treated subjects from literature and science to sociology. He created, in the world of Spanish medicine, a great new school of research. He was a lover of the arts, and his knowledge and his theories, original and personal to him, found expression in such celebrated works as his *El Greco y Toledo,* published in 1956.

His talents and his activities, so remarkable and so varied, brought him honored membership in the Royal Academies of Language, the Sciences, Medicine, History and the Fine Arts. This membership in five Academies is unique in Spanish history. He was the first Spaniard ever to be elected to the English Royal Academy of Medicine and to the Institut de France.

Politics, in the strict sense, was never a voluntary part of his life. Politics sought him out and imposed itself upon him during the final years of the dictatorship of Primo de Rivera. The public conscience at that time was at its lowest ebb, presaging the fall of the dictatorship and the final critical years of the Monarchy.

His sense of responsibility as a leading figure in the country's intellectual life led him then to assume a decisive participation in the political life of Spain. It was at this juncture that Ortega y Gasset, Pérez de Ayala and Gregorio Marañón founded the "Group to Serve the Republic" *(Agrupación al Servicio de la República).*

After the 14th of April, 1931 — the day the Monarchy fell — and with the obvious bankruptcy of the republican régime, this group of intellectuals refrained from all political activity. And it was at this time that the group's leader, Ortega y Gasset, uttered the famous words: "No, no; it is not this; it is not this . . ." *(No est esto, no es esto . . .").* It was, indeed, not the republic which might have been, not the republic which they had wished.

Five years later, on the 18th of July, 1936, the National Movement came into being.

During the civil war, Gregorio Marañón — Commander of the Legion of Honor — lived in Paris. There, during those days which have such dramatic historic importance for every Spaniard, he wrote *Liberalism and Communism in Spain.* The essay was destined to have an impact upon the thinking world of the utmost importance, for it revealed the profound causes which underlie, and justify, the national rebirth in Spain.

Liberalism and Communism in Spain, written in 1937, retains intact its warmth and realism, its clarity, and, above all, its value of scholarly analysis. The attentive and probing American reader will himself be the judge of my statement. The essay may even help in the understanding of certain events in the western world that are taking place today, and I am sure my Father would have warmly appreciated the title given to the American edition of his work, *The Liberal in the Looking-Glass.*

Gregorio Marañón not only was an enlightened, gentle spirit, he was one of those rare personalities who give to their fellow beings the example of a life which has been guided by a sense of work and duty, and by a glowing and unselfish love of country.

Multitudes stood mute at his interment, on the 27th of March, 1960. Professor and student, general and private, aristocrat and laborer, followed his cortège in the thousands through the streets of Madrid.

The day was cold. From the heavens a fine, gentle rain fell on the people of Spain, and mingled softly with their tears, and hid them.

Madrid
July, 1963
GREGORIO MARAÑÓN, JR.

THE LIBERAL IN THE LOOKING-GLASS

BY GREGORIO MARAÑÓN

Translated from the original French by Denise Loire,
in collaboration with John Howland Snow

I

THE SPANISH REVOLUTION AND WAR demonstrate a fact that has been true of all great historical events: While they are taking place, and for a long time afterwards, they are judged through mere incidents, themselves historically unimportant and seen through personal or partisan eyes. These incidents, nevertheless, do hold a clue to the true meaning of events.

I do not claim to be exempt from this unconscious and almost inevitable failing. Yet my effort to deal dispassionately with the subject does possess a certain substantiation. I have never belonged to what may be called a political party; my scientific background has trained me to coldly factual observation; and, above all, the naturalist, as a matter of principle, recognizes the ever-present possibility of error.

To the politician, the acknowledgement of a mistake seems humiliating if not suicidal. The scientist, on the contrary, knows that many of the things he once believed to be true are subsequently proven false, and that an unceasing search for truth requires that he discard each succeeding error with utter rigor and simplicity. This attitude of mind becomes eventually a pure reflex; one becomes quite impervious to the accusation of former friends that he betrays them, and to that of his former enemies that he is no more than an opportunist in their midst.

Lenin, the great disciple of Machiavelli, whose philosophy, far from being typically Latin, owes much to the Orient, said that in politics a fidelity to the past often posits a betrayal of the future. This maxim, like many others of Machiavelli, can be accepted only on condition that something be added, a something that had importance neither for Machiavelli nor for his disciples, namely: Ideas and theories may be flexible only when justified by constancy in conduct.

It is characteristic of all politics, everywhere, and in every more or less Machiavellian age, that it operates and juggles with theories while utterly disregarding any morality which might be involved. For the scientist, on the other hand, conduct is everything. His own is dictated solely by his yearning for truth. He is completely indifferent to all else.

II

WERE ONE TO ASK a hundred people, Spanish or not, the reasons motivating their favorable or unfavorable attitude toward one or the other of the parties at war in Spain, "a hundred" different answers would be received. Some people would voice their faith in democracy; some, their conservatism; others, pro- or anti-military leanings; still others, their Catholicism or their absence of belief. A few would perhaps even declare an intellectual leftist neo-Catholicism (this curious species of today's ideological fauna). Many would be moved by their horror of the executions and aerial bombardments, or even by their like or dislike for the leaders of the several parties. Few indeed would base their position upon the truth which lies behind the struggle, and say: "I support the Reds because I am a communist", or, "I am with the Nationalists because I am an enemy of communism."

This is the crux of the problem. Upon this premise one must focus attention, and upon it must inevitably be based his analysis.

My political competence may be contested, and I would not attempt to dissuade any who deny its being. My competence as an eyewitness to the political events within my own country during the last quarter of the century, cannot, however, be questioned. Nor can I be denied a competence which stems from the fact that I never once held political office, and that I have adhered faithfully to my principles of conduct — to, in other words, my conscience. Not one of my compatriots can with impunity deny that, though material disadvantages have ensued, I have held to my belief that the duty of an intellectual is to not keep silent, but always to be ready to offer his testimony when occasion demands.

III

SPAIN, FOLLOWING THE RESTORATION of 1874, experienced many years of peace (the colonial and the African campaigns were hardly full-scale wars) and many years of freedom. It was a freedom which seemed less than perfect, but nothing comparable is enjoyed by any people, anywhere on earth, today.

It was during this era of peace and freedom, as seems true in all such periods in history, that the strength of the State began to weaken. From this deterioration of governmental strength the momentum of the revolution grew.

The spiritual awakening which characterized this era of Spanish life — and gave to it its glory — led finally into political demagogy, a development made yet worse by the sudden and unearned prosperity of the years of the first world war and the period which immediately ensued. The Spanish, by temperament exceedingly ascetic, are of all peoples perhaps the most vulnerable to the tempting corruption of prosperity. And thus it was that at the time of General Primo de Rivera's *coup d'état* in 1923 there existed among all classes of society a widespread feeling that somehow "Things have got to change." The strength of this feeling greatly facilitated the triumph of the dictatorship.

There was as yet no talk of Communism, or if there was it was gratuitous. The general unrest which made possible the dictatorship was symptomatic of an obscure disintegration. This hidden malady affected the whole of Spanish society, from the masses of the people to the most highly placed. It was a strictly national phenomenon. One of the eminent political figures of the time defined it as "a critical illness of the body politic." This gentleman, Don Antonio Maura, a conservative in title but at heart a reformist, tried to fight it.

For many years it was confined to Catalonia, where revolution was endemic. There, the victims of its ravages were regularly recorded in the yearly statistics, like those of typhoid. Already, fourteen years before, in 1909, the festering body politic had erupted, and a burning of convents and every kind of violence, in typical Spanish style, took place during what came to be called "The Tragic Week". Today, we have witnessed such great horrors that the events which caused so much indignation then seem little more than schoolboys' pranks.

It was not the street-rioting which constituted the importance of these events. Their grave significance lay in the fact that, for the first time, the Spanish liberal — now become the equal of his European counterpart — was fostering, by his liberalism, a profoundly anti-liberal cause.

This, ironically, was because its tinge was red. None of us could see it then.

Spanish socialism had not yet become an extremist movement. Indeed, a few years later it submitted with docility to the dictatorship of General Primo de Rivera. The only opposition to that régime came from middle-class elements. Some were of liberal leaning, many were life-long conservatives. And joined with this opposition was the most aristocratic group in the Spanish Army, the corps of Artillery. Even at the end of the dictatorship the heads of the Socialist Party would have accepted — of this I have irrefutable proof — a collaboration with a parliamentary monarchy reformed by a new constitution.

The visible communist influence, both in the fall of the Monarchy and the establishment of the Republic, was slight. Even the violent propaganda that preceded the elections of 1931 (which brought on the change of régime) shows scarcely a trace of communist influence. I do not believe that the word *communist* was once used during the fateful rally in the Madrid bull-ring a few days before the day of the elections. That very night one of the King's Ministers read the speeches and remarked that most of them were more moderate in tone than anything said, either by liberals, monarchists or government officials, at the time of the Barcelona riots twenty years before. General Mola, then head of Internal Security — the same General Mola who later became so very famous — gives a similar impression in his *Mémoires*. The men who held office during the final months of the Monarchy (many of them my personal friends) were well aware that the situation was grave, but none had the remotest dream of a communist menace. At that time it didn't exist at all.

The righest press, in its pre-election campaign, predicted catastrophy should the republicans win. To many, the warnings seemed far-fetched. The movement seemed of a most peaceful character, and its principals were moderates and liberals. Many of them, like Mr. Azaña, were devoid of all republican background.

It would be idle to argue on what might have happened had the Republic not been born. In my opinion, its coming was inevitable, the circumstances being what they were. But I shall not speculate, for there is one practice which is absolutely forbidden to the objective historian: Speculation as to what might have happened had not the events themselves taken place as they did. There is, however, no guesswork at all as to the accuracy of the prophesies made by the extreme right and the monarchists: Anarchy, unwarranted strikes, burning of convents, religious persecutions; and lastly, the exclusion from government posts of every liberal who, having backed the movement, would not condone its immediately resultant class-warfare. Those on the right who, in good faith, gave their allegience to the new régime but felt no special enthusiasm for its extremist republicanism, were not tolerated.

Thus were fulfilled the rightist prophesies to which the liberals had listened with a suicidal scorn. To deny this now is an inexcusable denial of the most elementary truth.

Several centuries of success in the governing of nations — with the English and North American democracies not yet to be referred to in the past tense — had imbued the liberal with an excessive, sometimes insolent, confidence in the superiority of his thinking.

Nearly every one of the statues in the cities of Europe and America, evoking from passers-by a reverence for great men, is inscribed with the name of a liberal. Yet, regardless of what the political future of Spain may be, it was the reactionary, not the liberal, who saw clearly the present phase of her history in its true light. On this point, the facts permit of no doubt.

But even the gloomy forecasts of those who predicted the breakdown of law and order were calculated upon the coming into play of such underground organizations as that, for example, of Freemasonry. Even to the most distrustful, any direct intervention by the communists seemed theoretical or, at least, extremely remote.

IV

MARXIST PROPAGANDA, whose beginning it is difficult to date with any precision, must have become intensified shortly after the new régime took office, as soon, in other words, as the weakness of the conservative elements in the new Republic could be assessed abroad.

I recall vividly a little experience of my own. One evening, a few days before the convents were set afire in May 1931, I happened to be strolling behind three men who were talking freely and loudly about politics. They were communists. Their tone of assurance, their utter conviction of triumph, were such that I might have been alerted — but . . . The belief in our national ideology, including that of our most progressive thinkers, was so strongly ingrained in me that I simply could not imagine a Spaniard who was not opposed to the totalitarian state. The day of the burnings opened our eyes.

The propaganda had been tremendous, and it had been largely under cover. The number of known Party members was small. At the first general elections only one or two communist deputies had been returned to office. How often did all of us not invoke this reassuring fact! But the three hundred columns of smoke, from all the cities of Spain, rising up toward the sky on the same day, almost at the same hour, in time of peace, with no provocation remotely commensurate with such barbaric response; these crimes which followed a technique of destruction admirably planned, and all unsuspected by the people of Spain, were tragic proof that an alien organization was here, and that it was making its first spectacular attempt to impose its rule.

For no personal surcease, but solely to record the truth, I am obliged to note that the sole protest heard from the ranks of the republicans at this time was one that I signed with two other persons, both of whose names are known throughout Spain.[1] No dynamic, concerted and effective intervention came from liberals in the face of these events.

Many Spanish people of liberal outlook had given their conditional approval to the Republic — to this new régime which, they hoped, would promulgate much-needed political and social reforms. And so necessary were these reforms that they are, today, an integral part of the nationalist government's program. It was to such a régime that had been extended hope and confidence, not to one dedicated to a policy of class-warfare, destructive and tyrannical, Marxist-style. Many of these liberals on this day[2] withdrew their confidence and support, and it is from this day that the slow agony of the new-born Republic began. They withdrew, I repeat, not because of the events themselves; they withdrew because the expected reforms did not materialize. For their years of hope and effort their reward was magnificent disillusionment.

Without the help of a "loyal opposition" within the government, and without the support of these "men of good will", the Republic was doomed. For a number of years the extremists on the left had ridiculed those who insisted that only by "broadening its base of support" with an impartial generosity, could the proposed Republic be firmly established. Today, these same extremists, in order to survive, are obliged to simulate before the world a deep regret for human values which they do not respect, including that of the Catholic faith.

The Spanish liberal is the victim of a significantly odd defect, a

---

[1]   The two men were José Ortega y Gasset and Ramón Pérez y Ayala.
[2]   May 11, 1936, less than a month after the proclamation of the Republic.

partial blindness which is common to all liberals, the world over. Because of it, he sees the anti-liberalism of the "right", yet is totally unaware of the anti-liberalism of the "left". The Spanish liberal also has a long-standing tradition of anti-clericalism, and this, while it enables him to see an anti-liberalism that is black, blinds his sight to the phenomenon when it is red. This has made him particularly vulnerable to compromise.

The liberal who is anti-clerical in politics frequently is perfectly orthodox in his private life. I once published some data, compiled while examining my patients, which showed that most of the men who wore religious medals belonged to leftwing middle-class parties. The French review which did the publishing inserted *right* where there should have been *left,* assuming a misprint in my manuscript. Yet these same leftwing sympathizers, wearers of religious medals, would blush with shame were they to fail to maintain in public that the burning of convents was for the good of the nation.

It is grossly unfair to attribute to no more than a few men the responsibility for this one catastrophe which foreshadowed so many others. The responsibility rests with each and every individual liberal in Spain, for it was he who failed to appraise the grave portent of events, who contributed to the assurance that they would not go unpunished, and who thus, by his willing connivance, destroyed what political stability remained.

From that time on the communist character of the Spanish unrest increased, its unfolding managed with consummate skill. At the time of elections and at public meetings, it was allowed to appear neither too powerful nor too alarming. Its strength always showed itself as less than in reality it was. At last, in October 1934, taking its cue from the rightwing victory at the polls, the communists attempted a revolutionary *coup de main* to take over the government.

This attempt is not remembered outside of Spain, where there is no particular reason for one to be acquainted with the details of Spanish history, even such a recent event as this. But Spaniards, who can not forget it, are apt to smile at the sudden self-righteous indignation manifested by those who did not scruple to wage revolution over a setback as legal as were the 1934 election returns. This self-righteousness is assumed, two years later, because a part of the population and the Army has risen, in its turn, in the wake of a ruthless abuse of power, including the assassination by three officers of the state police of the leader of the opposition party.[3]

These rebels of 1934 are the "loyalists" of today. And their assumption of the word *loyalist* beguiled many to extend them their sympathy and assistance from abroad. From now on it is much more realistic to speak of the two sides as communist and anti-communist, and to set completely aside the term "rebel". The use of this word raises at once the confusing question of priority.

The uprising in Asturias, in October 1934, was an outright attempt to put into effect the communist plan to take over Spain. Spain was not selected solely because of the peculiar susceptibility of a new régime, one which from the first had rejected all legal authority in this always unstable country; nor was it based solely on the old, worn-out and false cliché that there was an affinity of temperament between the Spanish and the Russian people. The choice rested equally on the fact that the triumph of communism in Spain would unquestionably, and with very little delay — because of geographical and racial ties — bring in its train a serious weakening of fascism in Europe and, most importantly, a rapid conversion to communism of most of Latin America. The initial, preparatory phase of this conversion — the takeover of American liberalism — was then already well advanced and is even more so today.

The communist attempt in Asturias failed by a miracle. But two years later, a second, more formidable attempt was made. That Red Spain, still at war today, is in a political sense absolutely and completely communist, cannot be doubted by anyone with two eyes who

---

[3] José Calvo Sotelo, who, on the night of July 16, 1936 was kidnaped from his home by members of the Government's Assault Squads and riddled with bullets. This act is generally considered to have been the immediate cause of the "Generals' Revolt."

has spent even a few hours in the country. Nor can the fact be questioned by anyone abroad, unless he deliberately chooses to view the Spanish political landscape as through a mirage, clinging in his own mind to the simple, but effective, illusions of liberty, the public good, democracy, or the new "constitutional republic" of Spain.

Now in the open, the militant communists no longer hide their purpose. Others in the government who are not communists but who are hopelessly trapped, still speak of defending a democratic republic because they know the extent of human credulity. Even they, however, will reveal in private that they maintain this false position because of intimidation, or because of a sort of ethical delusion that leads them to place friendship, or party loyalty, before duty to their own conscience. There is also the ever-present fear of liquidation.

As I write these words, Mr. Anthony Eden,[4] a man certainly above any suspicion of bias, attested before the world as to the imprint of Moscow upon the Spanish scene. No one, in good faith, can remain in doubt as to the fundamentals of the problem. My own undaunted liberalism, even now, cannot hold in any less respect those who, in all sincerity, are still able to condone this movement, or are able to give it their support — if it is actually their belief that through communism Spain and the whole world will find salvation. It can still be hoped that their allegiance and support — quite devoid of unworthy motives or intellectual insufficiency — are really based upon a love of liberty, social progress, democracy, respect for freedom of thought, and all the other noble ideals that have no connection whatsoever with the Bolshevik state.

V

WHEN I SAID A SHORT WHILE BACK that the number of communists in Spain was small, I was not in error. They were, and have continued to be, a minority. This is true even in the red trenches and among

---

[4] A high-ranking member of successive British governments who later became Sir Anthony Eden.

those behind the lines. Spain made the mistake, as do the countries of western Europe and America, of judging the social impact of an idea — in this case the communist idea — by the mere number of its supporters. If men had the wisdom to profit by the lessons of history, they would need only to keep in mind that the triumph of the Marxist takeover of Russia was accomplished by a group of Bolsheviks whose number was almost insignificant. But as man bases his individual conduct almost entirely on personal experience, the lessons of history have not had, and probably never will have, any appreciable influence upon the conduct of entire nations. What took place in Russia took place twenty years later in Spain: A few trained men, the activists of a highly organized and ruthless minority, gained absolute control of the peaceful majority.

How this victory was achieved is now evident. There was organization, and iron discipline. Tactical use was made of every political faction whose ideology was closely, or even distantly, related. Each was exploited without a scruple, and abandoned the instant its usefulness was ended. The procedure was Machiavellian.

In Spain, the parallel is distinct. The revolution itself was well under way and yet there were only a few communist organizations as compared with the number of groups to which the socialists, the anarchists, the syndicalists, and even the leftist republicans, belonged. Only two or three Ministers represented the communists in the revolutionary governments — today's included — and, as I have said, the number of their deputies also had been, and still is, small. Despite this, the communists not only succeeded in imposing their power over every faction in Spain, they reduced the socialist groups to impotence. Some of these were as powerful at the beginning of the régime as was that of Largo Caballero, the hero of the Revolution for many months. The anarchist and syndicalist masses, who until last April made up the street mobs and furnished the most important contingents of fighting men, were also reduced to impotence. The uncoordinated action of these elements was easily dominated by the strict discipline of the communists. At the opportune time, and in cold blood, these "friends of the people" proceeded to liquidate both the anarchists and the syndicalists, who (let it be said in passing) represent in our revolution the most authentic expression of the national temperament.

But this extraordinary victory would never have become possible without the help of one other force — one which previously had been exploited and shrewdly outwitted — the force of liberal thought. While the conquest of Russia could be made by the exclusive use of the working classes, that of Western nations would have been totally impossible so long as liberal thought was in opposition to it. It was liberal thought which had shaped all the great social crusades. It had dominated European and American thinking throughout the entire nineteenth century. Then, just as its star was waning, the European war, fought and won in the name of democracy, gave it new luster and authority. And to this was added the brilliance of the United States of America, now arrived at their zenith — a young and impetuous champion of democracy, albeit frequently impelled by the somewhat petulant enthusiasm of youth.

This, the newly-furbished force of liberal thought, was why, during the years that preceded the present agitation, communist propaganda specialized in the subtle conversion of liberals, all over the world.

VI

HERE IS ANOTHER CLUE to the problem. Were it theoretically possible to reduce the great upheaval in today's world to a single, outstanding cause, I would not hesitate to state that it is the immense error into which the liberals of the world have been led.

From earliest origin, liberals have represented the humanistic ideal, itself the most fecund of all ideals, both spiritually and in the realm of practical every-day living. And yet, most liberals now find themselves in sympathetic alignment with the most anti-liberal ideology that has ever existed on earth.

The liberal was, in essence, the tolerant, understanding man, convinced that the betterment of the world could not be achieved unless liberty were at its base. The modern era of liberalism really began with the Renaissance. At that time, political theory, and much of the thinking of learned men, was inspired by Tacitus, the great prototype of all enemies of despots, the first liberal in the classical sense.

Centuries of struggle against tyrants, however, stamped in the liberal mind two quite understandable but completely erroneous concepts. These were, *first,* that the enemy of liberty is always one and the same, the tyrant, the king; and *second,* that the liberal flame is found in the people, and is to be nourished by the fire of popular favor. The conseqences of these two misconceptions were first made evident by the French Revolution, fomented by the liberals against the despot, and in the interest of the people. At once, a new despotism, that of the People's Tribunal, sprang forth, and new dictators issued from the masses, from Robespierre to Napoleon. The true liberals were the inevitable victims, for they, faithful to their liberalism — not to an ideology, but to their own high principles of conduct — rebelled against the new tyranny and were forced into exile or sent to the guillotine.

At that time was born another species of liberal, destined soon to become the most numerous in the world by far. From birth, each member of the species was the victim of congenital daltonism. His greatest fear consists of not being *thought* liberal. He has no conception, in any depth, of the basic implication of true, classical liberalism, for the new intellectuals have kept from him the knowledge necessary to its understanding. To this new generation has not been shown *the conduct of* a liberal; he has only been persuaded that he must *be* one. The immense prestige of this socially-accepted liberalism explains his attitude, and excuses it. Even the most hardened of reactionaries cannot repress a smile of gratification (How often have we not observed it!) when someone says to him, "Deep down, you know, you really are a liberal."

The new liberal, on the other hand, just cannot endure having his liberalism questioned. Not to be liberal has come to imply, in people's minds, a lack of real intelligence. After all, many, many of history's greatest men, famous for their creative labors, either have been liberals or their philosophy has been deeply influenced by classical liberal tolerance. Not to be "liberal" now implies that one is an "enemy of the people" — a phrase which originated during the French Revolution* and still retains much of its first invective and prestige.

Finally, so many of the advances of our civilization having been made under the symbol of liberty, not to be "liberal" implies also not having a modern, progressive mind. There is a germ of truth in all this. Yet liberty can have no special "color" — red or green — nor is liberty a mere matter of conflcting ideas. It is a basic principle of conduct. What a fatal error that *liberty* has been debased to party politics, and, worse yet, to deliberately created class-struggle!

Communists, with shrewd intuition, have exploited these three weak points in the vanity of today's liberal, and have bent him to their service. Certainly the negation of all liberalism, fundamental to the structure of the communist state, should at first sight make extremely difficult its reconciliation with the true liberal idea. But the communist, like all great propaganists, is not deterred by contradictions. Well he knows that the capacity for collective credulity is practically infinite. Along with this general credulity, today's liberal entertains a peculiar *naïveté* when appealed to in the name of his dearly loved Utopia. In this respect, the compass of today's world is truly amazing. At the very moment when, in the Union of Soviet Socialist Republics, dissenters from the rigid creed of the government are exterminated by the score, and when the leaders of anti-communist parties are made to disappear, the liberal persists in his belief that the U.S.S.R. is the home of moral progress and liberty, the Mecca itself of liberalism.

---

* In his opera, *Andrea Chénier,* Umberto Giordano correctly ascribes this phrase to the Revolutionary Tribunal in its liquidation of countless "enemies of the people" during the reign of terror.

The extent of this *naïveté* in Spain is almost incredible. Even now, on the Red side, there are men of the most liberal eloquence and attitude who inveigh against the "dictatorship" in the *opposite* camp, while they themselves not only are not permitted to express their own thoughts, they are often obliged to publish in the public press whatever has been dictated to them. I experienced this myself.

Last November, in Madrid, a communist said to me (using the familiar form of address, *Tú),* "You have always been a liberal; naturally you will be with us." The very same day a Worker's Council had banned one of my books because in it I had written these eight words: "I have always been a liberal, thank God." When, upon leaving Spain, I commented that such a proceeding did not seem to me exactly "liberal", I was immediately labelled "an enemy of the people" — and a writer in one of the American countries (a communist and a Catholic) described me in print as "the new Spanish Torquemeda".

Of course, a great many liberals — all those not blind to red — and many sincere republicans, have severed their ties with Spain, precisely because Spain is a communist land. Theirs is an attitude of strict fidelity to their principles of conduct. They are publicized as "traitors to the people's cause".

The flight of these liberals from Spain is a severe blow to communists, one not easily parried by propaganda. Every attempt has been made to lure them back, without success. Even those who were persuaded to attend the Cortes at Valencia, so painstakingly planned, within twenty-four hours were back in France. The opinions they brought back they voiced in private. One opinion, however, has been so widely circulated that it can be quoted without fear of placing any of these men in jeopardy: "The régime of Red Spain is totally Marxist; a true liberal has no place in it."

VII

THE COMMUNIST MACHINATION presented another great danger for Spain — its internationalism.

Even the least traditionalist of Spaniards seems to retain a greater leaven of his national character than do most of his European counterparts. Yet Spain itself is a country of greatest contrast. I have on many occasions said that our regionalism is at once the most spontaneous and the most authentic manifestation of the inmost soul of Spain, reflected with unvarying unanimity in the way Spaniards who have emigrated to Latin America have grouped themselves according to the provinces of their origin. Across the Atlantic one speaks of Italians, Frenchmen and Germans, but when it comes to Spaniards the reference is to Castillians, Andalusians, Galicians, Asturians or Catalans. To me, it has always seemed that these great regional characteristics are far less political than they are biological. And I think it is a serious mistake, one which has been made by many people, to attempt to project into this noble regionalism the notion of separatism.

The very well-spring of Spanish patriotism flows from the sum total of this regionalism, itself a normal extension of the deep family loyalty which all our people hold so dear. And far from being weakened by regionalism, patriotism is constantly nourished by it, and made strong. In whatsoever village or city of Latin America, precisely as in Barcelona or Madrid, Spaniards come together in their traditional provincial groups, like big families, scarcely aware of their neighbors. But let the nation be threatened — by whatever cause — and all unite, love of *country* their catalyst. The present common danger may well prove to have been a blessing in disguise.

Much of the enthusiasm in today's Nationalist Spain is inspired by national unity in the face of an inspired Basque separatism. There, the ambition of a very small group has been grievously exploited as a tool of communist internationalism, a situation which has been most erroneously interpreted abroad. Catalonia, though officially in the Red camp, has on the other hand been wise enough not to fall prey to a similar manoeuvre. This fact is going to have repercussions at the end of hostilities and later. As for Navarre, whose Basque region temperament is exceptionally strong, it has in fact played the leading rôle in the present Nationalist resurgence.

When a separatist movement was attempted during the first Spanish Republic, by a group called *cantonal* (*i.e.,* "district"), the great orator Castelar lent all of his vast prestige against it. In a most famous speech, this man — who in those days was the very personification of Spanish republicanism and liberalism — declared himself ready to forsake democracy and the republic, to abandon the liberal cause, if only it would save the country. There are in Spain many leftists who know this speech by heart, and who quote it with emotion. Beside it, in beauty and in its finest modern application, Marxist Utopia pales to drabness and insignificance.

Two months before the onset of the Revolution I wrote an article which was published in a number of newspapers in Europe and America, in which I stated that if the newly organized Popular Front government failed to give to its ideology and its program a deeply national appeal, a national uprising would ensue. Little credit is to be attached to this guess. The open hostility of the Spanish people toward the clearly alien technique of the pre-revolutionary riots — never sanctioned by any of our several governments — was plain to see.

Then, as time passed, a profoundly significant indication of the correctness of my prediction could be discerned — though not a soul commented upon it in print. Its significance lay in the fact of a change in the outlook of the student bodies of our Universities. Students had formed the spearhead of the liberal forces in their fight against the dictatorship of Primo de Rivera; students had been active agents of the dissatisfaction that brought about the change of régime. Now, from the beginning of the third year of the Republic, their outlook changed. It changed with such rapidity that at the time of the election of the Popular Front a socialist professor, who but a short time before had been the idol of his students, now faced open hostility in his classrooms. He himself told me that most of the new generation of students were anti-Marxist, *i.e.,* they were Nationalists. There wasn't a one of us professors who couldn't have confirmed this, and today eighty percent of our students are volunteers in the Nationalist forces. Many of them were reared in an atmosphere of present-day liberal thought, and during their early school years had belonged to liberal organizations, including, in some cases, even socialist and communist ones. Some of these young men I knew in prison during the years of the dictatorship — they were scarcely more than children then — and today they are the heroes, living or dead, of the anti-Marxist cause. What impelled them to change sides — without the shadow of a doubt — was their realization of the anti-Spanish character of the Popular Front.

The communist leaders soon saw that this was the main strength of General Franco's movement. For this reason, their propaganda in the beginning of the war dwelt on the "outrage" committed against the people of Spain by the Nationalists' use of Moroccan contingents in the field. I was in Red Spain at the time, and I could see that this alien argument made not the least impression upon the Spanish people. They and the Moors had been comrades-in-arms for generations.

Only those who disparage the past and who disingenuously believe that history begins with their own intrusion, fail to appreciate the depth of meaning of all those exploits which together make the history of a people and nation. In Spain, those of an alien ideology failed to appreciate the bond created by such traditions as the campaign of *El Cid Campeador,* or the conquest of Granada which ended the empire of the Moors in Spain — accomplished, in part, with African troops. Every man of Spain who fought on the Red side felt far more close, ethnically, to the Moors in the opposing lines than ever he did to the semi-Asiatic forces of the Soviet who already were filling up the cadres of his own rear-guard.

Next came an attempt to discredit the Nationalist resurgence because of the use of foreign troops. The Red leaders, on their part, once they had become convinced of the necessity of giving their men a national motivation, pretended to change the communist war into one of liberation. As might have been expected, this pretension was far more successful abroad than it was in Spain. A people who have lived surrounded by Russians, French, Czechs, etc. — and who know from personal experience the value of their help — cannot feel too disturbed that foreign soldiers are fighting on the other side as well as on their own. There is not one Spaniard but knows that the war he fights is no civil war, but an international struggle to the death. And not one, Red or Nationalist, has ever in his wildest dreams imagined that this foreign help could become "occupation" of his homeland, once the war was over.

Spain well remembers her war of independence against Napoleon — a highly popular war whose spirit the communists would dearly like to revive. Victory and independence were won with the help of a formidable English army, led by one of the greatest generals of the century. With the defeat of Napoleon, Spain remembers, the friendly army and its general left the country, retaining not a single foot of Spanish soil.

Nor is the Spaniard apt to forget that during the European war of 1914-18 the English and the Americans occupied whole sections of France, only to depart as soon as the victory was won. No one in Spain entertains the slightest doubt that the goal of the international troops now fighting on both sides of the Spanish trenches — those fighting with the Reds, and the Italians and Germans fighting with Franco's divisions — is far removed from mere territorial conquest. This invasion, so alarming to people abroad, does not alarm Spaniards at all. Were any one of the nations whose soldiers are in Spain to attempt to seize one inch of Spanish soil, Marxists and anti-Marxists would immediately unite, and face the enemy with the same terrible courage that they are now pitting against each other. As for that one piece of Spanish rock taken by the English so long ago, at a time when our national consciousness was dormant, there is not a Spaniard who still does not dream every night of Gibraltar.

The important thing is not the temporary aid given by foreigners in men and material. That question could be resolved outside of Spain by a few statesmen. The important thing is that aliens have attempted to capture the mind of the nation.

Were there not a single soldier, not one Muscovite gun, on the Red side, the crux of the matter would remain: Ideologically, Red Spain and Red Russia are the same.

As for the Nationalist side, were the Italians and Germans to be numbered in the millions the spirit of the people — with all its virtues and its shortcomings — would still be all-pervading, more devoted than ever, utterly and infinitely Spanish.

It is futile to attempt by sophistry to conceal this vital truth, for it is an absolute. And upon this absolute, even before the war started, had been measured the strength of one side, and the weakness of the other. If *Arriba España,* the stirring war-cry uttered with so much feeling by many a non-Fascist Nationalist today, had been adopted by the forces of the Marxist state, their chances of winning would have been, by this gesture alone, immensely enhanced.

VIII

THERE, IN SUM, are the precise terms of the challenge. It is a struggle whose outcome is fraught with momentous meaning for all of humanity.

On the one side is a régime, anti-democratic, communist and oriental; locked with it in battle is another régime, anti-democratic, anti-communist and European, one whose final form will be molded by an all-powerful Spanish reality. Just as in the fifteenth and sixteenth centuries Italy and the Low Countries were the scenes of struggle between great powers whose victory or defeat would determine the shape of Europe, so today two great ideological forces of the world clash in Spain. This time it is Spain that bears the tragic burden, and for a victory which must benefit all. This is her glorious mission.

It is upon these terms that Spaniards have faced the challenge. It is upon these terms that the distant spectator in other lands should take his position, too, for he may become far less of a "distant spectator" than seems possible to him today.

The communist formula is unique; with it is being attempted, by new and unorthodox methods, the conquest of the world. Nor is the anti-communist formula necessarily fascist. Italy, Germany, Portugal and Japan are anti-communist; openly or more guardedly, many of the other European and American countries oppose the doctrines of Marx. Yet, though sharing certain basic principles in common, each one governs itself, in its own way. Clearly. there is choice.

Without the perturbing presence of the modern liberal element, the problem would be clear-cut. Liberalism's immense prestige, and its colossally unfortunate blunders, have filled with confusion today's political scene. Its utter blindness to the anti-liberalism of the left has been pledging its soul to the devil.

The liberal's punishment will be equal to his error, for liberalism, as a political force, will in all probability exercise little direct influence on world affairs during times which soon will be upon us. True liberalism, however, will remain, for it is a *spiritual* force, a personal code of conduct. By whatever name it may be known, true liberalism, from its origin and by its essence, reflects the immortal drive toward the betterment of man and his estate, the deathless spring of human progress.

Some day, and without a doubt, true liberalism is destined to rise again, purified, from the ruins of the dictatorships of today.

The liberals of Spain now know the truth. Other liberals, elsewhere in the world, have yet to see the handwriting on the wall. I do not write to persuade them. To a thinking man, conversion does not come from suasion but from his inner conviction; and whoever is thus easily persuaded must always be suspect. Not so the one whose whole inner being has been through the fire which tempers his soul.

The day will come when the hosts of the liberals, everywhere, will hear the thunder, and be startled by sudden light, and, forsaking a crusade bereft of its illusion, they will find anew within their conscience the high ridge road to eternal truth.

BACKGROUND

The political and social background in Spain which led to the convulsion.

BY DR. EDWIN F. KLOTZ

Edwin F. Klotz, formerly professor of Spanish and History at Chaffey College, Alta Loma, California, earned his doctorate degree in Philosophy and Letters at the University of Madrid, 1954-57. His dissertation, *Los Corsarios Americanos y España: 1776-1786,* was published in 1959 by the University of Madrid, in collaboration with the Del Amo Foundation of Los Angeles. In 1963 Dr. Klotz was appointed an Administrative Consultant in the State Department of Education by Dr. Max Rafferty, Superintendent of Public Instruction for the State of California.

THE SETTING

TO THE HOME OF Dr. Gregorio Marañón in the early afternoon of April 14, 1931, came Count Romanones,[1] Secretary of State to His Majesty, King Alfonso XIII of Spain. Romanones' mission was no secret to the small crowd who watched his arrival from the street. He had come to negotiate the surrender of the ancient Spanish Monarchy to the titular head of the Republican Revolutionary Committee, Niceto Alcalá Zamora.

It was an historic moment. Three liberals, in private session, were altering the course of a nation's history. For the second time in fifty-eight years, Spain was to have a Republic proclaimed without the loss of a single drop of blood.

King Alfonso was to leave the country that very day. The Republicans were to form a Provisional Government.

When the conference ended, Romanones returned to the royal palace, convinced he had saved the nation from bloodshed and civil war. Both were yet to come.

Five years later, mid-wife Marañón was forced to flee to safety from the very Republic he had so tenderly helped guide into the world. From his exile in Paris, the conscience-stricken intellectual wrote *Liberalism and Communism in Spain,* first published in the *Revue de Paris,*[2] December 15, 1937. Bravely, Marañón told the unvarnished truth about the conflict which raged from 1936 to

---

[1]   Alvaro Figueroa y Torres was made Count Romanones in 1907. The personification of the liberal monarchist, his historical works, his memoirs and his political contributions are published in three volumes: *Obras Completas,* Editorial Plus-Ultra, Madrid. (No date is given, though I know they appeared around 1960.)

[2]   *Liberalisme et Communisme:* EN MARGE DE LA GUERRE CIVILE ESPAGNOLE. *Revue de Paris,* 15 December, 1937. Republished in book form, Paris and Madrid, 1961. First American edition, 1964.

1939: The Second Republic had created a Soviet Spain.

Moreover, he said, intellectual liberalism was largely responsible.

Marañón returned to Franco Spain after the war. When he died in March, 1960, the entire nation mourned his passing as it had mourned no man since the death of Manolete, the great matador. Dr. Gregorio Marañón, the liberal who had so materially helped in the birth of Socialist Spain, died a hero to the Nationalist Spain which followed. His funeral cortège lasted the greater part of a day. It was attended by Ministers of the Franco government. University classes were suspended. For weeks, eulogies of Marañón resounded from the platform and in the Spanish press. As one editor wrote, "Not only Spain, but the world, has lost a most exceptional man."

His passing was a "rude blow", lamented the Director of the Spanish Academy, Menéndez Pidal. And one of Marañón's old friends of republican days, Ramón Pérez de Ayala, declared that his baptismal name would rank with that of a wise and holy Pope, Gregory the Great.

How does one account for the acclamation of an entire nation for this great liberal, a man who had been personally and directly involved in the destruction of the old régime? One answer is that Marañón was a warm and friendly personality; his sincerity was above reproach. But in the wider, in the historical, sense, it was his honest declaration that what had happened to Spain sprang from an innate "color blindness" among liberals (including himself) toward the subtle menace which, so unconsciously, they had embraced. The people of a reborn Spain saw in his *Liberalism and Communism* the "examination of conscience" which was lying, latent, in their entire generation. Marañón's magnificent self-indictment* of ". . . the immense error into which the liberals of the world have been led . . . [an error which carried us into] sympathetic alignment with the most anti-liberal ideology that has ever existed on earth", struck home.

The reference was all too poignant, all too clear. All of Spain had

---

* Page 30.

lived through the blood bath. Marañón's message was an important one, to Spain directly, to all the world by parallel application.

Marañón, unlike his friend José Ortega y Gasset, was not politically inclined. By profession he was a doctor of medicine, his specialty being endocrinology. He enjoyed an international reputation as an historian. He was never a journalist, which Ortega y Gasset at times certainly was. And unlike the latter, he was not a proud man. He was emotionally detached, and was not quick to assault. He was humble, restrained, pensive, rational. His heroes were not Voltairian. His mind had not been so intimately trained as was Ortega's in the schools of philosophical German pessimism. The one term which best described Marañón, and the one the most preferred, was humanist. He employed this word frequently, and his humanist tastes are evident in the choice of people about whom he wrote: Juan Luis Vives, friend of Erasmus; Padre Jerónimo Feijóo, the eighteenth-century monk whose reflections stimulated an entire generation of Christian-oriented reformers; Gaspar Melchor de Jovellanos, known widely as the Spanish Jefferson of his day.

In this essay, a lingering, liberal vocabulary is often evident in the choice of words, and Dr. Marañón's phraseology at times reflects that of the environment in which he moved. As an intellectual, he respected the trained intellectuality of others. And it was this acceptance which led him, quite without his realization, into ways not consistent with true science. In the words of his repentance, it rendered him "color-blind".

Many paths had led to the holocaust of 1936-39, and Marañón, the humanist, trod one of them, the byway of liberal Spanish thought. Yet his was the only liberal school to declare its tragic error when confronted by the brutal reality which ensued. Many of his former friends and colleagues chose to fight for "democracy" under the Red banners. These were the socialists, the anarchists and the radical republicans. Men like Marañón and Ortega y Gasset refused to take part and fled the country. These men accepted the result of the war; the radical republicans did not. They do not accept that result to this day. Why?

We shall find the key to this enigma in an examination of Spanish liberalism.

THE LIBERAL HUMANIST

A HUMANIST is by nature conservative. By this I mean he is an intellectual aristocrat who advocates a structured society, individual self-discipline, and prescribed freedoms. When he steps out of his study into the world of politics, he sees a world of passion, and promptly prescribes the remedy: Reason. Plato did it. St. Thomas More did it. Ortega y Gasset did it.

Ortega's views are well expressed in *España Invertebrada,* a work which preceded by some years his famed *Rebellion of the Masses.*[3] "The mission of the masses is none other than to follow the best", he proclaimed. Thus reasoning, Ortega looked at Spain, looked at the contemporary world, and saw that the masses had rejected the traditional minority which so long had governed them. Thus, he wrote, "Where there is no minority which acts over the collective mass, a mass that knows how to accept the influence of a minority, there is no society."[4]

The remedy thus prescribed by Ortega — an aristocracy of intelligence to govern the untamed masses — was not new. Marañón himself, in the Introduction to a book written by his friend, Marcelino Domingo, formulated the idea this way:

> "It must be intelligence [wrote Marañón], that is, knowledge, comprehension, clarity, tolerance, which exercises the necessary civil power over every Spanish community. It must be a disinterested and generous hegemony, because its goal is not, as in other dictatorships, its own perpetuation, but rather its own and desired liquidation as a result of the success of its efforts."[5]

[3] *España Invertebrada.* Revista de Occidente, Madrid. 1955 edition.
[4] *Ibid.,* p. 94.
[5] Marcelino Domingo, *¿A Dónde Va España?* Madrid, 1930, Prólogo de Gregorio Marañón, p. xvi.

The humanist of the school of Marañón or of Ortega is thus not philosophically opposed to a dictatorial government so long as it is "generous" and run by "intelligence". But there is in Marañón's concept of the state run by "intelligence" an element which is far removed from Plato's image of a stratified republic governed by "philosopher kings". Marañón's dictatorship of intelligence would consciously "liquidate" itself. One wonders — though is it clear conjecture — if this philosophy was not employed by men who wanted to persuade Marañón and his influential friends of the "parallel" between it and the Marxist "withering away of the state". An intervening "dictatorship of the proletariat", in this case, would fall naturally into the sequence of events clearly desired by its proponents.

Marañón's own humanist liberalism preached a "revolution from above", a phrase made popular at the beginning of the century by the conservative, Antonio Maura. It was a solution in the enlightened Spanish tradition of benevolent despots. His socialist friends sought "revolution from below". Since both these revolutions seek drastic change there developed a "community of sentiment" among all the reformist and revolutionary elements in Spain. This desire for change permeated deeply all Spanish political thinking. It affected the entire basic structure of the nation, *i.e.,* the economic and social system as well as the Church.

Thus Marañón outlined his empire of intelligence with an "orientation towards socialism" in 1930 in a book authored by a future Minister of the Second Republic. In 1936 this Minister, Marcelino Domingo, did not see that his party was playing the game of a Kerensky. "If the Republic needs more advanced changes", proclaimed Domingo, "we will open the way for such new plans. Kerensky fell because he had to fall."[6]

The fusion of liberal and socialist humanists in the 1930's was an international phenomenon, and it is one which persists. The reasons can be traced, for it was the rationalism of the eighteenth century which led directly to twentieth-century liberalism and its

---

[6] *El Socialista,* official organ of the Spanish Socialist Party. Feb. 12, 1936.

color blindness. This is true whether the liberalism is that of a Lincoln Steffens in the 1920's, of a Gregorio Marañón in the 1930's, or of those who in the 1940's accept Ho Chi Minh's proclamation that his inspiration and guidance were the French Revolution and its "Rights of Man". It is true also of liberals who, like Herbert Matthews of *The New York Times,* saw Fidel Castro as the George Washington of a new Cuba.

In Spain, what tied the community of sentiment together was a theoretical system of life and thought called Krausism.

KRAUSISM

HISTORIANS WHO TODAY study the impact on Spain of Karl Christian Friedrich Krause (1781-1832), are astonished that this third-rate German philosopher should have become the preceptor to several generations of Spanish intellectuals.[7] Krause succeeded (at least to the satisfaction of his followers) in weaving together a system of "higher" morality out of Kant's reason, Hegel's idealism and Rousseau's sentimentalism. He called his system *Panentheism.*

Central to the theory was the hypothesis that "God contained the world without being exhausted by it." God was not a person; He was known only to the individual conscience. God originates within the individual, not from without. Christ was a symbol of human perfection; he was not God, or of God. Man, made in the image of God, could become perfect and return to God only in one way, by creating a perfect society here on earth. When man achieved this, he would "merge" with God.

One disciple of Panentheism wrote in 1883:[8] "The doctrine of

---

[7]   That is, historians of a conservative bent. J. B. Trend and Salvador de Madariaga write favorably of Krausism. Its critics look to Donoso Cortes and Marcelino Menéndez Pelayo, who, in the last century, recognized Krausism as a somber cloud hanging over human understanding. (See especially Menéndez Pelayo's *Historia de los Heterodoxos Españoles,* Tomo VI. Consejo Superior de Investigaciones Científicas, Madrid, 1948).

[8]   H. Giner de los Ríos, in a Foreword to G. Tiberghien's *Krause y Spencer.* Librería de Fernando Fé, Madrid, 1883; p. 10.

Krause possesses the excellence of being practical in the highest sense: That is, it is applicable to life in all its manifestations. As a complete system it embraces everything, the created and the uncreated, God and the cosmos, man and society. All rational ends are developed and are treated according to the ideal organization of human society: art and science, religion, morality, law, the beautiful and the useful, the just, Truth, the Good . . . everything comes under and is protected by the cloak of such a vast and organic theory."

Nothing can better explain the "two Spains" for the past hundred years than the institutionalization of these ideas in a predominantly Christian state. Already, twenty years before de los Ríos wrote the words just quoted, a university professor, Julian Sanz del Río, had refused to swear to protect the Crown, the Dynasty and the Catholic Faith. For this refusal to take the customary oath, del Río was summarily dismissed. Other professors resigned from their posts in protest, and these "Krausists", or free-thinking professors, then established their own "Free Institution of Learning", the goal of which was to "Europeanize" Spain. They would train an élite which would lead Spain forward into the stream of history. And they succeeded.

In 1931, it was largely adherents of this philosophy who captured control of the Second Republic. When disaster finally overtook them, Krausism as well as the Free Institution of Learning and its reputation, were destroyed.

Krausism, is must be emphasized, was not just a philosophy; it was a theosophic system. It was a way of life. As far back as the 1870's Menéndez Pelayo quite properly called it a sect. The purpose of the Free Institution of Learning itself was to "produce a personality such that it shall spontaneously comply with law." The technique was not to mold the student in the matrix of tradition and custom, but to "free the spirit" from the corrosive past. Books, therefore, were not needed to help mold character, for justice and good are realized from within. Virtue and sin are judged by the individual himself. Kindliness and self-expression bring out the best; authority and discipline are repressive, and do not.

All of this was set before the people of Spain as a progressive orientation, designed to carry them by its direction into the modern world. Upon the basis of inarticulate discontent its appeal came with soothing ease, for incorporated in Krausism was the assuaging sentimentalism of Rousseau: "There is no perversity in the human heart; the first movements of nature are always right."

What lay behind this color blindness of Spanish liberalism, therefore, was what Donoso Cortes dubbed the "immaculate conception of man."

Of course, few men of the world, and no orthodox Christian, could subscribe to such a doctrine. And it is one of the peculiarities of Spanish liberalism, and of the progressive republicanism that grew out of it, that few of its leaders were men of the world, as we understand the term. They were intellectuals. Menéndez Pelayo's description, written in the 1870's, fitted perfectly the republicans of the twentieth century: ". . . they would help and protect each other in their chosen profession. When in commanding posts in the University, they would divide the 'Chairs' among their own followers as if they were so much conquered booty. They would not only speak alike, but they would dress alike and even adopt similar external mannerisms."[9]

There was unity behind this new mysticism. Perfection of society was its goal. To achieve this, Krause had enlisted the International Order of (Grand Orient) Freemasons as the instrument to carry his system around the world. In Spain, the Free Institution of Learning became something of a recruiting center for Freemasonry. Out of this came the political configuration of twentieth-century Spain: Through Krausism, Spanish Freemasons carried Rousseau into the age of Karl Marx.

The Krausists themselves accepted a community of sentiment with Marxists, and with all the followers of the socialist ideal. Two major theses were held in common: *First:* Man is perfectible; *second:*

---

[9] *Heterodoxos.* Tomo I; p. 385. *(Opus cit.)*

A change in social and economic conditions will bring about this perfectibility.

The Krausists and their Masonic friends saw their community of sentiment with the Marxists in this light. What they were blinded to were the fundamental intellectual contradictions inherent in the postulates of Marx and the socialists, despite the fact that those contradictions, which they themselves shared, were constantly pointed out to them by such reputable and intellectual conservatives as Donoso Cortes, Jaime Balmes and Antonio Cánovas del Castillo.

SPANISH FREEMASONS

MARAÑÓN MENTIONS THE MASONS in this essay only in passing, but he does grant the correctness of the fears of "reactionaries" in their regard, a fear held for many decades. (And incidentally, a word of caution is appropriate here lest the reader gather, for the moment, that these references to Spanish Freemasonry are somehow applicable to Masonry in England and America. No. The differences between them are legion, and historic.[10] Some of those differences will soon become apparent.)

Ostensibly, the goal of Spanish Freemasons has been the complete freedom of all beliefs. Yet, by their own decrees, and by the official acts of their Ministers when in power, religious orders have been suppressed, and Church lands and works of art appropriated. Their programs have called for enforced military duty of seminarians, the reduction of churches to a predetermined number, the abolition of celibacy on the part of the clergy, and the secularization of all cemeteries.[11]

---

[10] See William J. Whalen, *Christianity and American Freemasonry*. Bruce, Milwaukee, 1961.

[11] See Mariano Tirado y Rojas, *La Masonería en España*. Madrid, 1892. Tomo II; pp. 172-3. There is a whole library of books on Spanish Freemasonry written by Masons, ex-Masons, and non-Masons, and I have used the two-volume work by Tirado y Rojas because of his frankness and because its date of publication puts him personally beyond the reach of critics. For details of the period we are discussing, see *The Spanish Arena*, by William Foss and Cecil Gerahty. The Right Book Club, London; no date.

Many of these programs were successfully imposed upon the Church after 1931 and the inauguration of the Masonic Republic. It has been called so because, although the Provisional Government of 1931 did include two Catholics (Alcalá Zamora and Miguel Maura), all other posts were filled by socialists and Masons. The Grand Master, Martinez Barrios, became Minister of Communications; Marcelino Domingo, of Education; Álvaro Albornoz, Minister of Public Works. Indalecio Prieto, Largo Caballero and Fernando de los Ríos were all socialists, and all were Masons. Lastly, there was Alejandro Lerroux, a Mason and a professional conspirator for two generations.[12]

It was this assembly of men which sat idly by on May 11 — less than a month after the fall of the Monarchy — while the systematic destruction of churches and convents, by the hundreds, in every part of Spain took place. It was this wanton, and totally unexpected destruction, which gave rise to the popular liberal cry: "No, no; the Republic is not this!"

The breakdown of public order has been a part of Spanish life for almost a century. Yet few governments ever turned their backs upon the maintenance of essential public order as did that combination in May, 1931.[13] The destruction was enormous. Pictures give the impression of a nationwide bombing raid. Miguel Maura, a liberal Catholic who had been alerted to the plan forty-eight hours before it erupted, was actually forbidden by his colleagues in the Government to call out the Guardia Civil to attempt to maintain order. With grief and shame, Marañón describes the "three hundred columns of smoke".

"All the churches in Spain are not worth the life of one republican", commented Manuel Azaña, then a newcomer in politics but

---

[12] See José Plá, *Historia de la Segunda República*. Destino, Madrid, 1940. Tomo I; p. 108. On the other hand, Hugh Thomas, in his *The Spanish Civil War* (Harper Bros., New York, 1961; p. 27), names only five of them as Masons. He hardly mentions the destruction of the churches, and remarks (p. 28) that "Masons cannot be regarded as of major political importance at this time."

[13] José Plá, *Ibid.*, p. 122, adds a behind-the-scenes description.

destined to become the second President of the Republic. And Azaña's words apparently reflected the general attitude of the Government.

The events of May, 1931, were no more than a beginning. Five years later, in the summer of 1936, there commenced the murder of over 7,000 priests, nuns, monks, and other members of the religious establishment, including twelve bishops. The sole reason for this specialized genocide was that the victims were members of the Holy Catholic Church.[14]

Masons were among those responsible, yes. But this is secondary to the major point, which is that the Government, whose personnel was predominantly Masonic, did nothing to stop the destruction or to apprehend those responsible. No one was ever prosecuted. Not a single court record is available to assist the historian; he may only speculate on the infamous acts and on the names of those who committed them. Marañón seems to believe that the communists were responsible, but the evidence largely discounts any real Soviet-inspired leadership at that time.[15] Eduardo Comín, laying the blame directly on the Masons, offers no data to substantiate the charge.[16] The anarchists, who are those generally guilty of such atrocities, must have had some brilliant direction, for the blood bath and destruction were not only well organized, they were timed to a specific day in three hundred widely scattered parts of Spain. José Plá witnessed many of the events, and was so stunned by the Government's passive attitude that he wrote, "They [the Government] not only witnessed the burnings, we can almost say they presided over them with a determined indifference."[17]

More than one historian has stated, and with apparent objectivity,

---

[14] For an exhaustive compilation of the names of the victims of religious persecution during the Civil War, see Antonio Montero, *Historia de la Persecución Religiosa en España, 1936-1939*. Biblioteca de Autores Cristianos, Madrid, 1961.

[15] See David T. Cattell, *Communism and the Spanish Civil War*. University of California Press, Berkeley, 1955; p. 63.

[16] Eduardo Comín Colomer, *Historia Secreta de la Segunda República*. Editorial Nos, Madrid, 1954. Tomo I; pp. 152-3.

[17] *Op. cit.,* Tomo I; p. 122.

that a hatred of Christianity is but one aspect of Freemasonry in Spain. If the interpretation of ex-Mason Tirado y Rojas is accepted, the Order considers itself a religion superior to all others and that it is destined not only to supplant all other religions but to abolish the rules of law and order and of property which rested upon those faiths. This parallels the writings of Krause.

As preached by the disciples of Krause, the panentheistic concept of mankind postulated that in order to create a new man one must start by destroying man's old institutions. Hence, the law, property and religion of the "old" man are anathema; they oppress. Tirado y Rojas remarks that, at least for Spanish Freemasonry, "Of these three enemies, religion must be the constant object of our immortal attacks, because no people have ever survived their religion, and by killing religion we will have at our disposition the law and property, and we will be able to regenerate society, establishing upon the cadavers of these assassins [of human rights] a Masonic religion and law and property."[18]

If this describes the direction and purpose of Spanish Free-masonry, then the actions of the Masonic Republic are intelligible. And so is the fusion of Masons and Marxists as expressed in the person of the Grand Master, Martinez Barrios, who was destined to become the President of the Republic-in-Exile. Campaigning on the Popular Front program in Seville during February, 1936, Barrios appeared on the platform with socialists, communists and anarchists, and in a hall studded with red flags, and symbols of the Soviet, declared that ". . . we are together."[19] That night, when he departed from the screaming crowd with the communist clenched-fist salute, the several rocky roads of Spanish Liberalism merged, to form a freeway to victory at the polls, then, leading onward, to the sudden abyss of war and destruction. As with the socialists, the anarchists and the radical republicans, the liberals of the Martinez Barrios school have yet to acknowledge this incontrovertible fact of history.

[18]   *Op. cit.,* Tomo I; p. 170.
[19]   As reported in *ABC,* Madrid's famous monarchist newspaper, on Feb. 15, 1936.

They continue to fight for their cause.

This is the fundamental difference between them and the Marañón's of our day and age, in every country, and under every flag.

SPANISH SOCIALISM

SALVADOR DE MADARIAGA, in 1930, wrote that "the Socialist movement in Madrid is thus the only truly historical entity in Spanish modern politics; that is, the only feature endowed with an inner life which gives it a permanent, growing and formative value in the life of the country."[20] Of those very men who were to turn Spain into a Soviet satrapy in 1936, Madariaga sadly observed: "Every one of the leaders of the Left . . . Largo Caballero, Prieto, Azaña, Besteiro, Fernando de los Ríos, Araquistan, Negrín, Del Vayo, were old acquaintances or friends of a lifetime. It was in these men that I, like every other liberal or socialist Spaniard, had put my trust."

Marxism had entered Spain during the period between 1868 and 1876.[21] It came as a two-pronged movement. In the big cities, the First International organized workers into a strongly centralized unit called the *Unión General de Trabajadores (UGT)*. In other areas, and in the south, Marxism followed the divisionist route laid down by Mikhail Bakunin (with whom Marx and Engels vigorously disputed). The Bakuninites were generally decentralized, and openly violent; the Marxist unions organized by Pablo Iglesias were institutionalized. By the 1920's, they had reached such acceptance and respectability that they cooperated actively with the dictatorship of Primo de Rivera. By different means, the two movements worked

---

[20] *Spain: A Modern History.* Frederick A. Praeger, New York, 1958; p. 145. I have written *1930* because this passage from the 1958 edition is identical to that in the 1930 edition published both in English and in Spanish. (The rôle of Salvador de Madariaga as an interested interpreter of modern Spain might well be a topic of research for some graduate student, preferably a conservative. The reader himself might compare, for instance, Madariaga's preface to the 1943 edition of *Spain* with that of the edition brought out fifteen years later, particularly where it touches on Russia.)

[21] There is a detailed study of this by Maximiano García Venero, *Historia de Las Internacionales en España.* Ediciones del Movimiento, Madrid, 1956.

toward ends essentially the same: Destroy the Monarchy; destroy the Church; destroy Capitalism. One addition could be made to the list: Destroy culture itself.

As the Communist *Manifesto* of 1848 had announced the views and goals of Marxism, so the Paris *Commune* of 1871 suggested to Marxists the tactics which would achieve proletarian power. Lenin recognized this. And so did a famous Spanish conservative, Cánovas del Castillo. Cánovas was the Great Restorer of the hereditary Bourbon kings following the revolutionary period of 1868-1874. He was more than a politician; he was a political theorist. He analyzed the Paris *Commune,* he studied the declaration that Marx made of the event, he watched the succeeding proclamations of the Workingmen's International, and he came to a precise conclusion: "The International," he declared, "impelled by socialism, impelled by the passions of the working classes, from the moment they lose faith and are blinded by the exaggeration of the equalitarian principle, will arrive at the most monstrous aberrations that anyone could imagine in the world up to the present time. It is impossible to deny, considering the facts [he continued], that the International is the greatest danger that human society has ever encountered."[22]

In two lengthy speeches before the Spanish Cortes in 1871, Cánovas del Castillo insisted that the criminal nature of the International made it illegal before the law. For a time his pleas prevailed. But when the liberal Monarchists gained power in the mid-1880's, a new law made legal the operation of the International and its subsidiaries. By 1886 *Casas del Pueblo* (People's Houses) began to mushroom in working-class neighborhoods. Here, in these socialist centers, the workers were indoctrinated with a barrage of hate propaganda. The steady development of this process was made light of by a great many respectable people, but Benito Pérez Galdós sensed acutely its ominous overtones, and declared, "We are sitting on a

---

[22] The two speeches, entitled LA INTERNACIONAL, are included in Cánovas del Castillo's *Problemas Contemporaneos.* Madrid, 1884; Tomo I.

volcano."[23] "Not only that", Galdós observed "we have both feet in it."

Measured as were his words, to all intents and purposes they went unheeded by those who might have made the years to follow far less unhappy for the people of Iberia.

El Socialista appeared, the official organ of the Socialist Party. Its very first issue (March 12, 1886) declared that the workers must organize themselves "separate from all bourgeois political parties".[24] The Paris *Commune* was held up as a shining example of militant revolution in action. Two weeks later, on March 26, a letter from Friedrich Engels appeared, extolling the objectives of the International. On the fourth of June there appeared a biography of Marx, who had died in 1883. At no time in all its history did *El Socialista* deviate from the proletarian revolutionary goals of Marxism. "As bad to call us monarchists as republicans", the paper declared in 1886. One year later *El Socialista* made its political intransigeance crystal clear:

"The Republic to which the working class aspires is the republic of work, that republic where economic and social equality is a fact; and that republic can only be socialist. Only the worker's party will be able to implant it in our country."

And this is how it turned out. Liberalism compromised with socialism to the hilt, a pattern which later was followed with acute similarity in Britain. When Largo Caballero, the successor of Pablo Iglesias, declared during the elections of 1936, "I am a Marxian Socialist, and Communism is the natural evolution of Socialism, its last and definite state", he not only sounded like a Fidel Castro, he was in strict conformity with the goals set forth by Iglesias and Engels in the 1880's. Álvarez Del Vayo was also explicit in *El Socialista* on February 7 of the same year (1936): "You have to follow the straight path until you erect a new socialist society, just as it has

---

[23] *Política Española; Obras Inéditas.* Madrid, 1924.. Vol. IV; p. 271. RENACIMIENTO.
[24] I am grateful to the Hemeroteca of Madrid (Plaza de la Villa) for access to the original issues of newspapers referred to in this presentation.

been raised in the sixth part of the world: in the Soviet Union." The socialists' "example and their guide", declared Del Vayo, should be none other than Rosa Luxemberg, the Spartacus communist who failed (with Karl Liebknecht) in the bloody attempt to take over a prostrate Germany in 1919.

Another in whom Madariaga had put his trust, Indalecio Prieto, showed clearly enough that, should the socialists gain power, he was hardly averse to the totalitarian technique of purges. In the April 23 (1936) issue of *El Socialista* he thundered against Melquiades Alvarez as a turncoat, because this important politician switched from republican to monarchist. On May 1 Luis Araquistan called Melquiades a traitor. In the massive slaughter of the following August, Melquiades Alvarez was among the first to be assassinated by the People's *Chekas*.

Salvador de Madariaga himself nearly perished at the hands of self-appointed militiamen who took him for a different Madariaga, a member of the opposition. Like Nehru in our day, Madariaga expressed simple shock and incredulity at the barbarism of a movement which others had tried to persuade him was utterly devoid of morality. Yet those "in whom he had put his trust" were no different in 1936 than their predecessors had been fifty years before. This, the liberal Madariaga could not see. With all the evidence of history before him, he was utterly convinced he could work with the "new barbarians" of the 1930's. Either he could not, or he would not, recognize his intellectual color blindness, and seek its cure.

SPANISH REPUBLICANISM

WHAT WAS THE GENERAL ATTITUDE of the Spanish republicans who were contemporary with these events? This question goes to the very core of Spanish liberalism, and of the infection which has been called its color blindness.

One basic fact is clear enough: While socialists rejected republicanism with a vengeance, as we have seen, *republicans never rejected socialism*. As Alcalá Zamora expressed it just a short time prior to the collapse of the Monarchy in 1931, "The republicans do not have to say that they are socialists because they accept socialism as a civilization; and if they don't call themselves 'socialists' it is because they understand that it must be a question antecedent to that which refers to the form of government. The discrepancy, as is clear, is not fundamental but of form. It does not mean that in the present circumstances republicans and socialists are not united."[25]

In that same month, Rafael Sanchez Guerra, son of a former monarchist Minister, joined the ranks of the republicans, declaring, "a republicanism that does not respect the advance of socialism is not republicanism." He went on to say that "even supposing that Communism should come to Spain, would it do anything worse than what the [Primo de Rivera] dictatorship did?"[26]

Today, Rafael Sanchez Guerra would have little trouble in answering the question. A long period of self-imposed exile cured his particular blindness, and a few years ago he joined a Spanish religious order in a zealous expression of the repentance felt by many of the generation of Marañón for the problems about whose proposed resolution they had been so mistaken.

Two primary points make Spanish republicanism foreign, both in content and in application, to what Americans would naturally gather from the term. One is the amorphous conception of a republic woven into the designs of Krausism; the other springs from the fact that Spain was traditionally a legitimately constituted Monarchy.

Let me develop these two points separately.

The men of the Second Spanish Republic looked to the heroes of the First as their idols and inspiration. Thus Alcalá Zamora, in his inaugural speech in the Cortes in 1931, claimed that the men of the First Republic (1873) had left "two guides which will make [our] failure impossible: on the one hand they stand out from above as shining lights of our ideals and as pillars of rectitude. On the other, here, in the rush of events, they have marked the pathways of danger with the anguish of their sad and selfless explorations."[27]

---

[25] *El Liberal*, Madrid. Oct. 2, 1930.

[26] *El Liberal*, Madrid. Oct. 21, 1930.

[27] Eduardo M. Del Portillo and Carlos Primelles, *Niceto Alcalá Zamora, Vida Intima y Política de un Jefe de Estado*. Madrid, 1932; p. 120.

The experience of the First Republic was indeed bitter, but, considering its utter failure, it would hardly seem to us a "shining light". When the Revolution of 1868 succeeded against Queen Isabel II, the generals and politicians attempted, two years later, to create a "democratic Kingdom" by "electing" an Italian Prince, Amadeo of Savoy, as King Amadeo I. Within two years Amadeo abdicated in confusion. The republicans then proclaimed the First Republic. A majority vote of the Cortes confirmed the "will of the people".

The bloodless coup soon turned to anarchy and civil war. In the brief ten months of its existence, the First Republic had four presidents and seven cabinets; it never agreed on a constitution, and it seldom governed over more territory than the small area around Madrid.

This essay into democracy was such a disaster it seems incredible that its example and its leaders, two short generations later, should be held up as the idol of all Spanish republicans. Yet one of the first acts of the Second Republic was to name the largest street in Madrid after the Catalán lawyer and historian, Francisco Pi y Margall, second president of the First Republic and leading exponent of the "federal" principle. Pi had defined his goal as "a synallagmatic Republic commuting with the eminence of Justice in Humanity and the pure motive of its naturalness in God, until it finds the fundamental synthesis of the self."[28]

In Pi's republic the condition of harmony among men would assure a mighty pyramidal structure of sovereign communes throughout the land, all bound together by voluntary contracts and by free association. The central government would be but an agency representing their collective will. Sovereign authority rested in the communes. There would be no police force, but an identity of interests;

---

[28] The reader familiar with Spanish may want to try his own luck with the original text: "Es la República Federal una República sinalgamática commutada con la eminencia de la Justicia en la humanidad y el puro motivo de su naturaleza en Diós y hasta encuentra la síntesis fundamental del yo." Quoted in Conde Romanones' *Obras Completas*, Tomo I; p. 678. *(Op. cit.)*

no law, but a collective force; no classes (of people), but a functional division of jobs.

The oddities observable in this Utopia seem, at least in retrospect, entirely in keeping with such thoughts. Pi y Margall early declared himself a socialist, and frankly stated that his form of democracy was quite compatible with Marxism.[29] Engels recognized this at once, and styled Pi y Margall as "the only Socialist among the official republicans, the only one who realized the necessity of basing the Republic on the support of the workers".[30] Yet the heart of Pi's "federal principle" was extracted verbatim from the works of Pierre Joseph Proudhon, the same Monsieur Proudhon whom Marx literally annihilated in his *Poverty of Philosophy,* published in 1847. I myself think it would be accurate to say, about these Spanish socialists, that not only did Engels misjudge that peculiarly Spanish product, the *mélange* of socialism and Krausism, but the Spanish Krausists themselves badly misunderstood the coldly opportunistic nature of Marxism.

A WORD, NOW, about the second point I mentioned: Spanish republicanism's conspiratorial nature and history.

Political conspiracy, while commonplace in Europe both before and since the French Revolution, has been totally alien to the American concept of politics. Indeed, it is so alien that the vast majority of us Americans simply do not understand it at all. I have always felt that this itself was the major reason why so many of our citizens were led to support the Abraham Lincoln Brigade during the Marxist civil war in Spain between 1936 and 1939. The Brigade, recruited here in palpable violation of our own and of international law, was to help the Spanish "Republicans". This designation was

---

[29] See Pi's *Historia de España en el Siglo XIX.* Barcelona, 1902. Tomo V; and Romanones' *Obras Completas,* Tomo III, p. 60.

[30] *Revolution in Spain.* International Publishers, New York, 1939. Marxist Library, Vol. XII; p. 318. THE BAKUNINISTS AT WORK.

enough to gain widespread financial and moral support for results which were, and were designed to be, the precise opposite of what the word itself conveyed.

The conspiratorial movement called Spanish republicanism began in the 1790's, in the days of the brash José Marchena. The movement had been at war with monarchism in Spain since the French Terror. As the wave of the future it carried with it many of the finest liberal minds of Spain. Despite history and its blood baths, this wave still fascinates no small number. Gregorio Marañón became one of the most distinguished exceptions.

It was from the anarchy of 1873 that the two kinds of republicans characterizing the Spanish scene, emerged. One, the *possibilists,* were led by Emilio Castelar, who one day wished that a republic might be possible in Spain. The other was the *activists.* The activists for the remainder of the century carried on revolutionary plotting and "liberating" expeditions from the safety of France or Portugal. Count Romanones in his younger days was interested in such efforts and even corresponded with the disillusioned rebel republican, Ruiz Zorilla, offering to join the cause.[31]

The organized, violent form of republicanism did not gain much momentum until the appearance, at the turn of the century, of a man who was to become the "Conservative" Minister of the Second Republic, Alejandro Lerroux. An exhortation of his in 1906 is indicative: "Young Barbarians of today: Plunder the decadent and miserable civilization of this country without a future. Destroy its temples, put an end to its gods. Lift the veil of the nuns and raise them to the category of mothers in order to improve the race. Crash open the public Registrars of Property and make a bonfire of their papers so that the pyre can purify this infamous social structure. Go into the humble places and raise legions of proletarians so that the world may tremble before its alert justices. One must re-do everything . . . Go! Go! Do not hesitate even before graves or

---

[31] Conde de Romanones, *Obras Completas.* Tomo III; p. 27.

altars. The Church must be destroyed. Fight! Kill! Die!"[32]
Lerroux organized his Young Barbarians.

The fruits ripened in their season. In 1909 a series of strikes, a "bloody week", took place. Most of the violence centered around Barcelona, Lerroux' political home. Nuns and priests were attacked, and some thirty religious houses burned. The arrest and trial of one anarchist responsible, Francisco Ferrer, made into a *cause célèbre,* brought about the fall of the conservative government of Antonio Maura. One disillusioned Lerrouxista subsequently wrote that the League for the Rights of Man and the Masonic Lodges in France were alerted to promote an international campaign in favor of Ferrer.[33] Whoever was behind it, the campaign was a success. An atmosphere sympathetic to the anarchist was created not unlike the atmosphere which in our own day grew from the efforts through the press in favor of Caryl Chessman, or the atom spies, the Rosenbergs.

The great Unamuno described these phenomena to a friend: "All the anarchists and anarchist sympathizers joined together. The *snobs* joined them and for months they would repeat the eternal arguments about the Spanish Inquisition; here in the most liberal country in the world! The fanatic Jew Naquet, the *snob,* Anatole France, the fatuous Paul Adam, the monstrous Rémy de Gourmont . . . all the international riff-raff. And they sing the song that Ferrer was executed for being a rationalist, and not as an anarchist. It makes you sick!"[34]

The year 1917 was a revolutionary year in Spain, as it was in Russia. For months the Government not only had to battle anarchists and socialists and republicans, but rebellions within the armed forces indicated the extent of the breakdown of the national structure.

---

[32] *Historia de la Cruzada Española,* edited by Joaquín Arrarás. Madrid, 1940. Tomo I, Vol. I; p. 45.

[33] José Rodriguez de la Peña, *Los Adventurosos de la Política:* ALEJANDRO LERROUX. Admon. de El Indiscreto, Madrid. (Undated, although the copy in my hands has an inscription by the author to the Marqués de Valdeglesias dated August 8, 1915.)

[34] D. Sevilla Andrés, *Antonio Maura, La Revolución desde Arriba.* Editorial Aedos, Barcelona, 1954; p. 363.

Anarchists in widely separated parts of Spain established "sovereign" units, as they had done back in 1873. Leaflets circulated throughout the country urging people to manufacture home-made bombs, to burn churches, business places, military barracks and court houses. "It is necessary to establish anarchist communism," said one of the leaflets, "in order to leave the earth free of human beasts. People: To Revolution!" A virtual state of civil war reigned for months before quiet was again established.

By 1923 the anarchy was so severe that Spain was on the verge of collapse. An organized murder campaign was aimed at the extinction of the whole bourgeois class. Bankers and businessmen were shot to death in their offices, or hauled out of bed in the middle of the night and assassinated in isolated places. In the twelve-month period between 1922 and 1923, over five hundred employers were murdered; one hundred and sixty of them in Barcelona alone.

Here is a brief synopsis of the chaos through which the people of Spain were living: Between 1902 and 1923 they saw thirty-three changes in government. In 1912 the Prime Minister, Canalejas, was assassinated immediately after he had settled a railroad strike. In 1921 the conservative Minister, Eduardo Dato, was killed. Antonio Maura was several times attacked. In 1922 and 1923 there were respectively 488 and 458 strikes of major importance. Terror and disorder then culminated in the Proclamation of General Primo de Rivera which established martial law and suspended the Cortes.

The dicatorship of Primo de Rivera, which Rafael Sanchez Guerra declared to be as bad as communism, was to be no more than an interim period in the prolonged social crisis. So long as the nation prospered, the General succeeded in pacifying the sectors of the economy which had the most at stake. His success lasted until 1929, when economic disorder appeared again. The republican-socialist-anarchist elements rushed to fill the vacuum left by Primo's retirement to exile in Paris. In August 1930, leaders of various groups met in San Sebastian and formed a pact. Three months later their

Putsch against the caretaker government of General Berenguer collapsed, and the leaders went underground or into exile. Alcalá Zamora and Largo Caballero went to the "model prison" in Madrid and from there continued to operate, calling themselves the Provisional Government.

Berenguer, nevertheless, lost his post. Admiral Aznar was appointed chief of state and the veteran liberal, Count Romanones, joined the new cabinet to oversee the collapse cf the Monarchy. Romanones felt he could settle the political crisis by calling first for municipal elections, and, later, for general elections to the Cortes. At the April 13 municipal elections the vote in the big cities, heavily in favor of republican delegates, was the signal for massive popular action. People poured onto the streets shouting, "Long live the Republic!" Banners, placards and signs appeared as if by magic, some of them lettered "Viva Russia!" Taxis and buses were commandeered by shouting and hysterical mobs. And despite the fact that the final count in those nationwide municipal elections returned 22,000 monarchist candidates as against some 8,000 republicans, the massive action in the streets, and the exaggerated importance given to the big-town vote succeeded in scaring the Monarch off his throne. The forces which might have guided the nation through the new crisis became demoralized and immobile. Police and military personnel were ordered to stay inside their barracks and not to fire on the crowds.

On the day after the municipal elections, while Romanones was negotiating the transfer of powers to Alcalá Zamora and his Provisional Government at the home of Dr. Marañón, the Minister of Interior (who was titular head of the state police) was unable to get to his office because of the crowds. His assistant, Señor Marfil, learned of the new government only at six o'clock that night when he saw workers pour into the patio of the Ministry. Two hours later, at the very moment that the King was leaving Madrid pursuant to the agreement, Alcalá Zamora and his co-revolutionists took over the security network of the nation. And not a shot was fired.[35]

The fate of this Second Republic was that of the First. It took a little longer, and the consequences were more lasting. The Second Republic boasted of two presidents and some ten governments in a little over five years, depending on when one stops counting the changes after 1936. To call this period one of instability is to employ a euphemism. It was constant civil war.

Anarchists paid little or no attention to the police of the liberal republic, and when the Right won the elections of 1934 the liberal republicans and socialists immediately plotted civil war. The result was the uprising of 1934, mentioned by Marañón in his apologia. It was not plotted exclusively by communists, as Marañón suggests, but communist elements were clearly engaged.

The socialist-anarchist-republican uprising of 1934 cost 1,330 lives and almost 3,000 wounded. Some 60,000 of the activists were put in jail. Full-scale military manoeuvres under the command of the Chief of Staff, General Francisco Franco, were necessary to crush the insurgents against the lawfully-elected government.

As fate would have it, however, the ringleaders who were caught and imprisoned as a result of failure in 1934 emerged as leaders in the national elections two years later, when the Left won by a slim majority. What followed is interpreted by some as tragic; by others it has been called a purification.

The Civil War lasted from 1936 to 1939. It left a million dead, another half million in exile, a nation in shambles.

As order gradually was brought out of chaos, those in Spain who felt that the blood purge had been necessary recalled words written by Angel Ganivet, a poet-diplomat of the last century. In a mood of

---

[35] The parallel between these events in Spain and the communist takeover of Czechoslovakia ten years later is demonstrable. See the topflight communist guidebook, *And Not A Shot Is Fired,* for the communist strategy to capture control of a democratic government by patient, and seemingly legal means. Translated from the Czech, it is now published in eleven countries. The U.S.A. edition is published by THE LONG HOUSE, INC., New Canaan, Connecticut. 1962. ($1.00)

pessimism just prior to the Spanish-American War of 1898, Ganivet said: "Faced with the spiritual ruin of Spain, one must put a stone in the place of one's heart, and even a million Spaniards must be thrown to the wolves unless we are all to go to the dogs."[36]

This stoic acceptance of alternatives has characterized the Franco state since 1939. Spain *has* recaptured her spiritual past. She *has* recaptured her dignity and independence. Spaniards feel that their million dead in that civil war set back the communist timetable for world domination by a whole generation. Spaniards are well aware that international communism has not forgotten this. Moreover, they are sensitive to the phenomenon noted by others alert to international affairs. Whereas the revolutionaries of the 1930's had enjoyed an international press whose unanimity of support was remarkable, the Government which emerged from those cruel years of Spaniard against Spaniard, and of Spaniard against Russian, found itself practically isolated, even ostracized, from Western councils.

Today, this is being corrected.

LIBERAL MONARCHISM

SINCE SPAIN TECHNICALLY IS still a Monarchy today, it seems proper to end our study of the varieties of Spanish Liberalism with a survey of that country's Liberal Monarchism. And the question which arises is this:

> Is the institution and continuity of the Throne subject to the majority vote of the electorate at the polls?

Count Romanones answered yes to that question in 1931, and the Monarchy collapsed. Monarchists of the Romanones school, in other words, became so liberal that they ceased to be monarchists in the traditionalist, legitimist sense.

Ever since the time of the Constitution of 1812 Spaniards had been arguing over the nature of their "written" or "unwritten"

---

[36] *Spain, An Interpretation.* Eyre and Spotteswoode, London, 1946; p. 41.

constitution. Traditionalists argued that a constitution is the collective law of the centuries; liberals argued that it had to be a written document. They were prepared to write one.

When the Cortes of 1812 met in Cádiz (at the time all Spain was occupied by Napoleon's troops) they issued a new constitution under whose terms the Cortes emerged as a single sovereign body representing the popular will. This constitution established a one-chamber legislature, elected by popular suffrage. It represented the spirit of Jean Jacques Rousseau and ignored the traditional method of representation by the three estates: The cities, the clergy and the nobility. This Rousseauistic alteration of the national tradition moved Gaspar Melchor de Jovellanos to warn: "A Cortes elected for one year would be able [under popular sovereignty] to undo in one day everything others had established in a century." He advised his countrymen that such a procedure would not lead to monarchy but to unbridled democracy: "If this dogma of national sovereignty can destroy today the Constitution you have sworn to, will not another legislature destroy tomorrow what you swear to today? What stability will your Constitution then have?"[37]

The Constitution of 1812 was rejected by the nation as a whole, yet its spirit persisted and the advice of the sage Jovellanos went unheeded. Between 1808 and 1932 Spaniards wrote, or proposed, at least eight new constitutions. As party succeeded party in political control, all too frequently by armed revolt, each attempted to impose a new one. This was the Rousseauist and the Krausist solution. The theory of an ordered society was reversed: Law was no longer its base; it was held that a model constitution would create a model state.

The device of the popular will, proposed in the Constitution of 1812, became operative with the importation of Amadeo I in 1870. It failed. The legitimate heir, Isabel's son, Alfonso XII, succeeded to the throne in 1876 and re-established the hegemony of the

---

[37] *Biblioteca de Autores Españoles.* La Real Academia Española, Madrid. Undated. Tomo 50; p. 377.

Bourbon kings. Yet as the years passed it was apparent that the thinking of the liberal monarchists of the Revolution of 1868 had not died. In 1931 the theory of the popular will again found a capable advocate in Count Romanones.

As a boy in Madrid, Romanones had witnessed the entrance of the Revolutionary General, Juan Prim, at the head of his troops following the overthrow of Isabel II. "He produced in me the impression of a supernatural being", says Romanones in his Memoirs, adding that General Prim and the liberal monarchist school became the model and inspiration for his entire generation.[38] Romanones' youthful zeal to fight alongside the rebel republican, Ruiz Zorrilla, has been noted.* He lived to preside over the surrender of the Monarchy to the victorious republicans at the home of Gregorio Marañón.

This political and intellectual orientation of men like Romanones is the key to many events, and I am not without regret that here is not the place to pursue the matter further. But I do hope that this brief discussion has helped to a clearer understanding of why Spain had a "monarch without monarchists" when the crisis came in 1931.

Conclusions

It has not been my intention in this brief analysis of Spanish Liberalism to suggest that all the blame for the disaster of 1936-39 rests with liberals. Certainly the collective Right, including the Church, must accept its share of criticism for its failure to cope with the fundamental economic and social problems whose expression was leading to violence for the very reason that they were not being faced.

My point is, and it is the core of Marañón's message, that the failure was essentially intellectual in nature. José Plá stated it correctly in 1936: "For thirty years, a ferocious, implacable criticism was produced daily without any appreciable letup, against the State,

---

[38] *Obras Completas.* Tomo III; p. 16. *(Op cit.)*
* Page 62.

against institutions, against the governing class and their best intentions to improve, and this criticism was carried out by the most gifted and most talented intellectuals of the nation."[39] No wonder historian Plá concluded that "the word intellectual came to be synonymous with revolution, in the strict sense of the word. It is impossible to imagine in this period a Spanish intellectual, near or far, who has not served the cause of anarchy."[40]

My own intimate study of these years has served but to strengthen my belief that any true approach to the resolution of the problems which spring from the magnificent forces of change, must first be principled, moral. It must tolerate no compromise with men known to be unprincipled and immoral by conviction. Just as Spain suffered then, the world today suffers from the silence of those whose conscience calls unswervingly for principle and for morality. When a whole class lays aside deep-rooted principles and faith, the result is what Julian Bender called the betrayal of the intellectual.

No; the Republic of 1931 certainly was not the Republic of which Marañón had dreamed. Humanist and liberal, he recognized his errors, and repented.

Yet the outcome of the conflict of the 1930's is hardly intelligible unless we conclude that Romanones, too, was wrong. Spain was not a monarchy without monarchists; it was a monarchy without monarchical leaders.

Not all the victorious nationalists were monarchists, but the traditionalist monarchists of the rural areas of Spain — those who had returned a three-to-one majority over the republicans in 1931 — became the core of the Movement which governs contemporary Spain. Many of them were seasoned, uncompromising, authoritarian traditionalists, that is, nineteenth-century-style *carlistas* who strode into battle with the cry, "God, Country, King". It was they who, in

---

[39] *Ibid.,* Tomo I; pp. 26-7.
[40] *Ibid.,* p. 27.

the bloody weeks of August, 1936, saved the Generals' Revolt from defeat; it was they who emerged 100,000 strong on the side of Franco to sweep whole provinces from the control of the revolutionary Republic.

The Spanish Civil War was indeed a war of religions, of two uncompromising attitudes toward human life. Marañón realized the choice that had to be made. He praised the Nationalists for their courage to fight for that choice.

He then told the liberals of the world the choice they, too, would one day face.

That message is inscribed herein.

EPILOGUE

From Act III of the opera *Andrea Chénier,* by Umberto Giordano.

In this scene, the indictment dictated by the spy, L'Incredibile, and written by Chénier's friend Gérard, has been read. Chénier, surrounded by the Paris mob and facing the People's Tribunal, now responds.

Rendered from the Italian
BY JOHN HOWLAND SNOW

CHÉNIER

Si, fui soldato
e gloriosa affrontata
ho la morte che vil qui mi vien data.
Fui letterato,
ho fatto di mia penna arma feroce
contro gli ipocriti!
Colla mia voce
ho cantato la patria!
Pura la vita mia
passa nella mia mente
come una bianca vela;
essa inciela
le antenne, ali allargate
ad un eterno volo,
al sole che le indora,
e affonda
la spumante prora
ne l'azzurro dell' onda . . .
Va la mia nave spinta dalla sorte
a la scogliera bianca de la morte? . . .
Son giunto? . . . E sia!
Ma ancor io salgo a poppa e una ban-
    diera
trionfal disciolgo ai venti!
De' mille e mille miei combattimenti
è la bandiera e su vi è scritto: "Pa-
    tria!"

            (verso Fouquier-Tinville)

A lei non sale
il tuo fango, o Fouquier!
Essa ognora s' insola
immacolata.
Essa è immortale!
Non sono un traditore.
Uccidi? E sia! Ma lasciami l'onore.

CHÉNIER

Oh, yes; I have been a soldier, and have faced death as glorious as is vile the one you will inflict upon me.

Yes; I have been a man of letters, and have employed the utmost force of words against hypocrisy and its hypocrites!

I have raised my voice in song, singing always of the Fatherland!

My life has been pure and blameless, its image passing before my inward eye like unto some whitened sail. Heavenward point its stays, taut are stretched its spreads as though reaching ever onward, to eternal horizons, toward the sun itself which engoldens them; a spray-swept prow dipping eagerly to the azure of the seas, scattering liquid diamonds in its wake.

Is this winsome ship, o'erwhelmed by fate, to home upon the whitened shoals of death? And with myself aboard? If so, I shall not desert her.

For there will come others. And for them, before the fatal crash, I leap to the topmost mast, there to unfurl to the winds a triumphant emblem!

Behold the banner of thousands upon thousands of struggles by my dreamship; for there, on high, you see inscribed upon this emblem a single, thrilling word: *Patria.*

To Fouquier-Tinville, the Inquisitor, Chénier now turns, and cries:

This banner, O Fouquier, your foulness shall not besmirch; forever it shall remain unsullied, for the flag of Country is immortal.

No traitor, I. Yet if, withal, I am to be done to death, so be it.

But leave to me my honor.

THE PUBLISHED WORKS OF GREGORIO MARAÑÓN

MEDICINE

Investigaciones sobre el aparato tiroideo.
Once lecciones sobre reumatismo.
La doctrina de las seccreciones internas.
Manual de enfermedades del tiroideo.
Ginecología endocrina.
Gordos y flacos.
Estudios de fisiopatología sexual.
Las glándulas de secreción interna.
El bocio y el cretinismo.
Endocrinología.
Manual de diagnóstico etiológico.

ESSAYS

Tres ensayos sobre la vida sexual.
La evolución de la sexualidad.
Amor, conveniencia y eugenesia.
La edad crítica.
Psicología del gusto.
Crónica y gesto de la libertad.
Ensayos liberales.

BIOGRAPHIES

Enrique IV de Castilla.
Amiel.
Las ideas biológicas del Padre Feijóo.
El Conde Duque de Olivares.
Luis Vives.
Tiberio.
Don Juan
El Greco y Toledo.
Cajal.
El Empicenado visto por un inglés.
Antonio Pérez.

LITERATURE

Vocación y ética.
Crítica de la Medicina dogmática.
El Alma de España.
Raíz y decoro de España.
Españoles fuera de España.
Vida e historia.
Tiempo viejo y tiempo nuevo.
Efemérides y comentarios.
El libro y el librero.
Cuatro comentarios a la Revolución Española.
Elogio y nostalgia de Toledo.

If this book is not available locally, just send your order to THE LONG HOUSE, INC., Box 3, New Canaan, Connecticut, enclosing $2.00 per copy. Shipment will be made immediately, prepaid.

The LONG HOUSE catalog of exceptional publications will be sent to you *gratis* upon request.